# TALKING BACK

*poems by*

# REBECCA L'BAHY

*Finishing Line Press*
Georgetown, Kentucky

# TALKING BACK

Copyright © 2021 by Rebecca L'Bahy
ISBN 978-1-64662-674-8 First Edition
All rights reserved under International and Pan-American Copyright Conventions. No part of this book may be reproduced in any manner whatsoever without written permission from the publisher, except in the case of brief quotations embodied in critical articles and reviews.

## ACKNOWLEDGMENTS

Grateful acknowledgments to the following publications where some of the poems in this book first appeared:

*Brain, Child*—"What No One Ever Told You"
*Halfway Down the Stairs*—"The Girl I Was Speaks"
*Leon Literary Review*—"Fear is Your Passenger" and "A Matter of Time"
*Mom Egg Review*—"Ode to My Commute on the Fitchburg Line"
*Mason Street Review*—"The Argument" and "Talking Back to Jack Gilbert" (previously "Lawless Pantoum for Jack Gilbert")
*Writers Resist*—"Consoling My Poem"

Publisher: Leah Huete de Maines
Editor: Christen Kincaid
Cover Art: Sheri Glover, Instagram: @gloversheri
Author Photo: Andrea Seward, https://www.facebook.com/HabakkukPhotography
Cover Design: Elizabeth Maines McCleavy

Order online: www.finishinglinepress.com
also available on amazon.com

Author inquiries and mail orders:
Finishing Line Press
PO Box 1626
Georgetown, Kentucky 40324
USA

# Table of Contents

What No One Ever Told You ................................................................. 1

Ode to My Commute on the Fitchburg Line ........................................ 2

The Argument .......................................................................................... 4

A Matter of Time ..................................................................................... 5

The Bathtub ............................................................................................. 7

Fat Love .................................................................................................... 8

Nursery, Clothes, and Tea ..................................................................... 9

Love Stinks ............................................................................................. 10

The Interview ........................................................................................ 12

Some Questions .................................................................................... 13

Envy ........................................................................................................ 15

Consoling My Poem ............................................................................. 16

Fear is Your Passenger ......................................................................... 17

The Girl I Was Speaks of Courage ..................................................... 19

Talking Back to Jack Gilbert ................................................................ 21

The Incident .......................................................................................... 22

Wild Life ................................................................................................ 23

Late August Haibun ............................................................................. 24

Clouds Like Mountains ....................................................................... 25

Observation Room ............................................................................... 27

What to Expect: A Poet's Guide .......................................................... 28

# WHAT NO ONE EVER TOLD YOU

Sometimes you feel a rage build in you and it is only 7 a.m. You are feeding the dogs, the cats, making waffles, making lunches, barking orders: *Brush your teeth. Brush your hair. Get your shoes. Get your backpack. We're late, we're late, we're late.* You are so close to what you have been waiting for—three kids in school full-time, your own brain-space. You sit and stare at a wall. There is a rock in your throat, a bird in your ribs. You avoid the kitchen. Sometimes the whole house. Drive around in your mini-van unsure where to go or what to do. Something is missing from your day. From your life. *You should, you should.* But you don't. Then 2:30 comes too soon, and your six-year-old wants to play house. How about a board game, you suggest. With a board game there's no pretending, there's a beginning, an end. She starts to cry. She wants to play house! Why won't you ever play house? You yell something at her, something mean. She cries harder. You are her first love and you have broken her heart so you let her: cartoons, candy, salamanders in the living room. Look at her! Do you even see her? How she's watching TV upside down in a headstand, hair spilled out on the loveseat, spindly arms holding herself up? It isn't until later, after the final push through dinner and clean up, the whole bedtime routine, after you collapse exhausted into her bed for cuddle that you see: three new freckles on the side of her face, that hair, those arms, her tiny baby teeth. You were there when they came in. You were there when she chipped one on the driveway. You will be there when they fall out one by one. You have always been there, even while you were thinking, *What if.*

# ODE TO MY COMMUTE ON THE FITCHBURG LINE

Because on the platform I can feel
bird song on my face.
Because alone with others is best
all of us quiet, waiting—
for the eye that casts its light
upon the weedy track, anticipating
a blast of inexplicable wind
that smells like water left behind
after lobsters have been pulled
from the pot,
and the conductor's accent—
that's no parody of Boston's working class
but sounds like it should be:
*Ay-ah Next! Ay-ah!* comforts me.

Because inside the car,
where the horn's muffled blare
sings its one long note,
I slide in next to Walt Whitman,
happy to rest my head
against the hard seat, give up time
and be where no one knows
or can find me.

Together in silence
we give praise to the world—
the tall grasses waving their feathered heads,
Thoreau's Walden in conversation with wind
and sky, followed by men
in hazmat suits, buildings marked
with misspelled graffiti
and someone's couch
abandoned in the trees.

It looks dry, inviting—
a nice place to sink into a poem,
when later I sit
in my windowless cube
and in my mind's eye
see us there—two parentheses paused
under a canopy of trees,
our tongues heavy
and wordless as stones.

## THE ARGUMENT

It's past dinner time and dark in Athens
Pizza, my face lit up by the menu
that hangs huge, like a sign
I should go big, get what I want for once
tuna sub, toasted, with crispy iceberg lettuce—
so, what am I doing? Over-thinking again
looking for a better choice,
some thing I didn't know existed, and I'm wasting
time God, I'm so hungry, I might lose my mind
everything smells so good, I almost wish
someone was here with me, whispering
sweet nothings like: *Go for it! You deserve it!*
*You only live once!* because suddenly I'm seeing tuna,
not the salad, but the fish
a school of those gray beauties
swimming fast, the ones in front breaking
through the surface of the sea
towards the indifferent sun,
blue sky, blue water, so much blue, it stuns
then the inevitable net, men
standing over their catch
in blood-stained coveralls,
stabbing with picks, going for the eyes,
stabbing the eyes behind my eyes
and there is thrashing, gasping, pain and surprise
that life should suddenly end like this, here, today,
when just minutes before all was routine.
Boring even. Then silence.
Gray bodies lined up on a concrete floor,
buyers, sellers, economics. The question,
as if on cue: *What'll it be?*

## A MATTER OF TIME

My father's new watch was utilitarian—
it had a round face, big gold numbers.
I admired its sweeping second hand.
I admired my father,
who since I was a little girl
set to work after dinner
washing dishes
though often times now
they don't get clean
just cleaner.

The last time I was here
I fixed the date for my father
or thought I had, until at noon
it flipped from *SAT* to *SUN*.
The watch had no regard
for my feelings of course,
no way of knowing my surprise
& frustration at its gears locked
in their own world of logic,
like my father—
who in the middle of my story
left the room to go trudge slowly
up the stairs, to count his pills.

That's when my mother, lying
on the couch mouthed the words,
*He can't tell time anymore.*

I remember my father.
In the '70s he had a garden
where he grew swiss chard
and marijuana.
I remember his thick black beard,
how one day he shaved it all off

and finding a strange man
in my bedroom, I screamed.
My father's smooth jaw opened
then and he bellowed: *That's the best
reaction I've gotten so far!*

It is quiet now.
My mother and I discuss
an exchange of analog to digital—
but in the end decide to let it be,
decide it's only a matter of time
before he forgets what a watch
is even for and we too
become just mouths and eyes
set on shiny faces.

## THE BATHTUB

was her reward for having made it
through another day of being our mother.

It had claw feet and no shower head,
was the reason for dinner at five,

the reason we were put to bed
too early. Place of soak and release,

her big toe added hot water in loud bursts
so my tooth brushing ran like a silent movie

in the foggy mirror, where the landscape of my mother's
breasts was warmed by a wet washcloth. I learned

by watching her how to push it down
under water, wave it with a lazy back and forth

of the wrist, like a flag of surrender, then stick it
back on her breasts, steam rising like smoke.

Was she sending out signals?
Asking the gods of motherhood how to become a woman

who could move through a day of house-wifely duties
with grace and ease? To become some other mother—

one who didn't need to pick up the phone day after day
ask anyone who would listen: *Do you have a minute?*

Sometimes after bath she would come to me
where I lay in bed still awake, watching the headlamps

of cars mark the ceiling and walls. I would breathe in her
baby powder smell and hope that she would fall asleep

with me there. I was a child and my need simple, basic,
plain. That she stay.

## FAT LOVE

Before you, love meant nausea—
ribs and hip bones, soggy cereal in the sink.

The morning headline read: *Vegetarian Leaves Majority
of Pasta Primavera on Plate.*

Before you, love meant waiting—
phone to ring, horn to honk, heart to break.

Today the kitchen smells like Moroccan stew.
At the supermarket, the checker knows us

how we pile our cart with color: orange, apricot, eggplant, lime
let the rinds of pears curl across the kitchen floor

decorate the curtains with Spanish olives,
sprinkle the sheets with cumin and coriander.

Ripping and tearing we use hunks
of French bread like sponges to soak up saffron sauce,

and for dessert crack open
pistachios and lick the salt from each other's wounds.

When midnight comes
we have candlelit breakfast in the bathtub

where there's no room for silverware or plates.
We marvel at the rolls of belly fat—

how comfortably they sit one on top
of the other, how easily a pinkie slides between.

## NURSERY, CLOTHES AND TEA
*For Mary Cassatt's Critics*

A girl's small dimpled body, white as kneaded dough,
stands loosely wrapped in a towel.

A black-haired girl slumps on a blue floral loveseat.
The picnic has been postponed due to a chance of triviality.

A lap dog dreams it's a wolf.
A woman wills the rain to end.

The forecast calls for more domesticity.
A mother with a daughter draped across her lap thinks.

Her thoughts of candle makers, masons, horse shoes,
and spices as unsentimental as a chair.

Working the needle, the thread, a woman stops embroidering
to sip some derogatory comments from a china tea cup.

A mother washes her small girl's feet.
Her labor as essential and dull as the white ceramic basin,

next to the pitcher splashing water without sound.
So much depends on the ambivalent door and

the breeze that finds the paint and dries it.
Now everyone is free to get up, leave behind

the long afternoon slant of sun, air fragrant with soap,
bodies pressed so close not even light comes between them.

Tell them Mary, where does everyone go,
once the paint has dried?

## LOVE STINKS

They closed our school
bussed us to the other side
of the city. Low enrollment they said,
but why ours & not theirs?
It wasn't fair. *Love Stinks*
by J. Geils was our favorite
that year, played on boom boxes
in the back of the bus as we scratched
our initials into the vinyl seats
past Mary Immaculate,
laughing at how the kids in our new
school were afraid of us, said we had lice.
The bus lurched along,
brakes squealing at the Purity
Supreme where our mothers shopped
for groceries, and where, as if possessed,
we all began to scream—
emptying our lungs with a sound so loud
drivers in cars with their windows up turned
to look. Our bus driver barely moved
her eyes from the road, she wore aviators
like Peter Wolf's, never told us
to sit down & shut up,
never said a thing
when one beautiful spring day,
a chant went up declaring *Jews suck! Jews*
whose invitations to mitzvahs
thick square envelopes, fancy writing,
parties with DJs and disco balls
would soon arrive by mail
inviting some, excluding
others though everyone was welcome
to join in the chant, was encouraged
even the little kids up front—why not?

It was a game, wasn't it? like the screaming
spontaneous, breathless, fun
it went on and on. After that I was sure
to sit by a window, look out—study
the way of front yards and maple trees
how their buds opened like fireworks—
exploding a heavy, sticky pollen
that coated everything yellow.
Was it just once? Just that
once?                    Yes.
And a lifetime of anticipation.

## THE INTERVIEW

The rooster on the cornflakes box
stares at me from his one eye
like he wishes he could fly
off his cardboard world to someplace good.
But if I'm not going someplace good
then neither is he, I tell him.

The briefcase does its job without complaint,
holds in my resume and the laughter
while the plants, wearing dust, pray for water.
But there are no clouds paid for in this apartment,
only electricity to run the fans
in the bedroom where I'm heated
arguing with my white blouse
who objects to the violation of being dirtied
up before the moon has even surrendered.

The sun follows my dwarfed body along the glass
walls of the industrial park. The highway's roar
beneath me doesn't cease
just because I've arrived in a new suit.

Afterwards, the littlest things please:
my key still fits the lock
and in the kitchen I eat a cheese sandwich
standing up, drink orange juice from the carton.
On the other side of the wall,
the plants are let down, clock ticks
as if embarrassed and from behind
the cabinet door, the rooster lets loose
with a cock-a-doodle-doo.

## SOME QUESTIONS

In that sunless corridor of replacement mothers,
was it my father's mouth that formed the words,
blowing them into the air like balloons
that floated and bumped before popping
leaving brightly colored scraps of latex
on the welcome mat: *Can you help?*

A kindly neighbor, yes, but who was she?
Was her hair the color of January,
gray clouds that hung too low?
Was she full of song like Mary Poppins?
Dressed in a black cape and twirling an umbrella
hoping for a mild day to take baby for a stroll?

Or was she more Cruella Deville in fur,
smoke curling from her lip,
thinking, *I'm not getting paid enough for this*
while baby lay in a back bedroom
stunned by the whiteness of walls?

Did she have the hands of a widow?
Bunions on her feet?
Did she smell like family, worry
about the jealous cat who hissed & skulked,
waiting for the sharp whistle
to erupt from inside the kettle's lonely quiet,
for his chance to pounce, to smother?

Yes, father was working, but did he rush
home to beat the earth's slow-moving rotation,
or were his feet halting as if through tangles
of underbrush, his car finding reasons
to make one more stop?

What was it like after the old woman
closed the door behind her?
Did father sleep with baby by his side?
Was he afraid of crushing her
during the long, dark, night?
Did they grieve together
for those large pink aureoles,
bulls-eyes marking the place of suck
contented sigh? Did baby root for them
on his clean white t-shirt,

did she cry out against absence
against loss, turn her cheek from the cold
bottle, its milk unsweet,
wailing now for those breasts
hard as stone
yet too tender for touch
boulders under a blue johnnie
that smelled of bleach
and opened in the back?

*No, my mother says now, No.*
*You have it all wrong.*

## ENVY

Your father tells you that if he had boobs
he'd give one to you every time you cried.

It's a gentle suck when you aren't too hungry,
so I don't blame him for the envy he feels

when you glue your blinkless eye on my face
the whites an unblemished robin's egg blue.

I wipe a drop of milk from your cheek
as your head droops under its own satiated weight.

I wonder what your father would have done
at the car repair shop where you were content

for nearly an hour to look at tires but then enough
was enough. Would he have walked you back and forth

until his breasts began to leak? Or would he have whipped
it out at the first whimper, right there in the dirty restroom?

## CONSOLING MY POEM

Imagine him at night, sleepless in his tacky golden bed.
How he tosses, turns, finally rising
at 3 a.m. to check his phone,
its glow a salve to his tiny soul.

What if it were you lighting up his screen,
what would you say?
Think hard, dear poem, be brave.
It's true you will never be appointed
member of the cabinet, plucked from obscurity
to be a confidant or aide—

you are a simple, humble poem
but forget all that now—
we need a hero
to hunt down the most powerful image,
wield words as if they matter, break lines
without mercy, and cast a spell so beautiful
it will do nothing less than save the world.

## FEAR IS YOUR PASSENGER

and today in carpool
driving the teenage girls home
after their NYC field trip,
you couldn't remember
the Statue of Liberty.
Not that you couldn't see her—
her masculine robed form
weather beaten green
vacant eyes like shades
pulled down over thought—
but the three words you needed
to name her floated somewhere
out there in the harbor—

out of reach and you flailed,
drowning for those words
the way your father does—

every conversation with him now
a game of charades
his hands pleading with the air
banging against the arm of the chair
when your desperate guesses
are useless and wrong.

How must it be to lose so much
so slowly
you can see it happening
so slowly
you are aware
of the losing
aware of everything moving
too quickly for you to follow
and so you choose to leave
the phone ringing
the dining room table

the television drama
throwing up your hands
exclaiming: *They talk too fast!*

You wish you could forget
the time you caught your father
watching a children's television show,
not just watching—engrossed in it
his mouth half-open
in concentration
and the awful moment
he caught you looking
and the mouth snapped shut—
both of you pretending
nothing had happened.

## THE GIRL I WAS SPEAKS OF COURAGE

Take my hand, she says
down these cellar steps

into the pitch dark.
It was you, remember

who turned out the lights
who wanted to feel all

your limbs tingle with anticipation
of bashed shin or skull.

You liked it down there
alone, no stars to guide you

liked to go deep into smells of must
and mold, past the crevices

in sandstone walls full of spiders,
past the shower stall, its soap

on a rope, hung cracked and dry,
past the tools on the peg board,

holding their metal breath,
that watched you move stiff and

zombie-like, arms outstretched
skin puckered gooseflesh

you wore proudly, relished
how alive you felt chancing the fall

a gash from hurrying towards
the bulkhead's sole crack of light.

Do you remember how you raised it up?
The quick duck, push, squeak of hinge

blast of sky, bright tree, air, sun.
Then doing it all again, just for fun.

# TALKING BACK TO JACK GILBERT

He was determined to have the life he wanted,
wondered why so many settle for so little
asked why we weren't more determined
to have a life that mattered. He believed we were

missing out. Settling for so little: family, houses, jobs.
Didn't we know we don't have much time?
He thought he knew what makes a life that matters.
My daughter tells me she wants real wings

so that she can fly. My daughter, my genie, asks me:
*What have you always wanted?* waits in the dark
for answers easy as wings. I feel myself running
out of time. Be greedy for what's inside you, Jack says.

Beside me under starred ceiling, my genie waits.
I reach inside, feeling in the dark for the right line.
*What have I always wanted?*
my heart thumps, hum-drum, hum-drum.

Have I become dreamless?
Jack said the heart can experience so much.
Tell me Jack, have I settled for too little?
The world is my daughter's sky and she wants wings.

Under the sheets I brush roots off my feet.
Jack turns his back on us, the conventional
house, job, family, believed they diverted
from what mattered. Ask me again why

I'm not more determined, have settled for so little.
I will show you how my fingers brush gently across
my daughter's back, how a pen becomes a wing
and the whole world our sky.

## THE INCIDENT

Why was he walking home
with me from the bus stop?
This boy who was a neighbor

but in no way a friend.
I try to remember
what I said or did to offend

but all that comes
is how quickly he turned and stung
my belly's softest spot.

*You better watch out*
 *or I'll tell everyone you're Jewish*
*& they'll throw pennies at you*

head buzzed as if full of bees
lungs and throat burned.
His venom sickened me.

Somehow I stumbled home.
*How did this stupid creature know?*
He was no good at school

or friends or sport but I knew
where he stood, always
knew when he'd washed his hair.

# WILD LIFE

The hunter leaves our bed early
to retrace his footprints frozen in snow.
Dressed in camo, bow across his back

he passes the dining room table
ringed with wine stains,
littered with crumbs from last night's meal.

Into the dark dawn he hikes,
drifting flakes of snow melting on contact
with his warm round face.

Up a tree trunk mottled with lichen
he climbs to his perch, sits for hours
in the quiet stillness of dawn.

From where I am, grounded at this low-down
level of wind-blown trash cans and dirty snow
I envy his birds' eye view

look forward to stories about the wildlife—
an owl's talons wrapped around a branch above
the wolf that freezes 100 yards out

when a tiny squeak from the hunter's shoe
reaches her ear. I picture his body pressed
against sky, how he blends colorless, waits

more animal now than man, his will
pitted against the hunger that drives
a mighty buck out into the open.

I can't help but hope
for a different ending for all of us—
no twitch of tail, no weapon raised

no punctured lung or heart—
just a man, cheeks flushed red
returning empty handed to his wife.

## LATE AUGUST HAIBUN

Despite our best spring effort—beds filled with soft peat, feet that step gingerly around first shoots of green—the garden is choked with weeds. Crab grass clings tight, bittersweet wraps itself round tomato stalks in tight spirals that reach into the air like wayward tails in search of a kite. From a distance, it looks like a Monet gone mad, an earthy mess of green, heart full to bursting. I pluck the last fruits of my labor, a cracked cherry tomato, its pulpy seeds spread across my tongue. *To every season*, I tell myself. The sunflowers, heads bowed, nod. But rather than console, the words leave me cold.

Pack of coywolf mourns a loss
I roll to my stomach in search of sleep
breasts pressed flat as moons

## CLOUDS LIKE MOUNTAINS

Same old commute
east to work
west home
index finger hovers
taps radio SCAN
button again and
again. Sun rises
sun falls, *No, it's the earth*
*that moves*
I know all
the words by heart
sing along
until I remember:
*I don't even like this song.*

Cars move
inch
by inch
last set of lights—
green, red,
green, dusk waits
hands on her hips
cows line up
at the barndoor
entrance

Then the highway
opens
its mouth gives breath
cars inhale
exhale
hit the gas
glance up to the horizon—
a habit of pavement
meets sky

Today a new line
dark and brooding
knocks me awake
gun metal mountains
reach higher
than memory—
crest of rock and trees—
almost black
a granite scab
blotting out
the Worcester hills—
not blotting
but raising them
up
into the sky.

## OBSERVATION ROOM

What am I if I love to watch the young
gymnasts through the glass?

If I envy the girls' lean defined muscles
pointed toes, their strength to kip and cast

to the high bar, giant once, twice, three
times before letting go—

tumbling through the air and landing with feet
that stick to the mat and do not stumble.

Who am I if I concentrate so hard
on the shirtless boy as he presses

his palms to the floor, legs straddling the air
ankles meeting with controlled touch, I feel

the pull of muscle in my own calves,
my own body holding that handstand?

Who is this middle-aged woman reflected
in the glass, magazine on her lap

whose body aches with such fierce longing
to defy gravity, shed

these sagging breasts, dimpled thighs,
leave observing behind and fly—

# WHAT TO EXPECT: A POET'S GUIDE

This poem was conceived out of boredom,
And this poem stole a pregnancy test from CVS.
This poem's water broke on the red carpet,
And this poem's labor lasted for years.
This poem was born once in a blue moon.
And after this poem, stitches and a blood transfusion.
This poem doesn't ever let me put it down,
And this poem stays in its room texting friends.
This poem was jealous of the one that came after it,
And this poem wakes me several times a night, afraid.
This poem won't eat anything but macaroni and cheese,
And when I put this poem in time-out it said it hated me.
When I carry this poem over my shoulder, it pats my back
And each night this poem must be nursed to sleep.
This poem was the most beautiful newborn I'd ever seen,
And this poem wasn't weaned until its 46th revision.
This poem wants to stay the baby forever,
And this poem always says: *just one more.*

**Rebecca L'Bahy** is a poet, writer, and teacher originally from the metro-Boston area. Her poetry has been published in various literary journals including *Leon Literary Review, Mom Egg Review,* and *Halfway Down the Stairs*. She holds degrees from Oberlin College (BA history) and Emerson College (MFA). Among her many jobs she has been an office assistant, paralegal, union organizer, reporter, bookseller, shoe model, gymnastics coach, and home daycare provider. Currently, she teaches in a public middle school and occasionally facilitates creative writing workshops in-person and on-line. The proud mother of three daughters, L'Bahy is married and lives in Worcester County Massachusetts. *Talking Back* is her debut chapbook. You can learn more about her work at RebeccaLbahy.com or following her on twitter @LaBlahMs.

www.ingramcontent.com/pod-product-compliance
Lightning Source LLC
LaVergne TN
LVHW041517070426
835507LV00012B/1637